THE BRILLIANT MINDSET OF
A REAL ESTATE AGENT

THE BRILLIANT MINDSET OF A REAL ESTATE AGENT

What It Takes to Achieve Your Goals

SHEILA ATIENZA

Privilege Digital Media

The Brilliant Mindset of a Real Estate Agent: What it Takes to Achieve Your Goals

Published by
Privilege Digital Media
Richmond, British Columbia
Canada

In this book, the author features fictional characters for purposes of illustration and presenting cases and situations. Any similarities to any person or persons, places, and events are purely coincidental.

Hardcover Book ISBN-13:
978-1-990408-01-4

E-book ISBN:
978-1-990408-02-1

Subjects
Business & Economics / Real Estate / Career
Business & Economics / Marketing / General
Self-help / Personality Development

Subject Categories
BUSINESS & ECONOMICS / Real Estate /
Buying & Selling Homes
BUSINESS & ECONOMICS / Careers / General
PSYCHOLOGY / Personality

Thema Subjects
Self-help & personal development
Property & real estate
Advice on careers and achieving success

CONTENTS

dedication

To you
who would like to explore
what it takes to achieve a brilliant mindset

inspirational quote

"Do not lose sight of a city
for one structure
or building
for in life
we may capture
charm, alluring view
that may not be obvious
but of value."

-Sheila Atienza, Author
Feed and Discern: Some Words of Wisdom, Some Poems, Some Life Lessons

INTRODUCTION

Introduction

Real estate, or shelter, no doubt, is one of the essential requirements for human survival. Whether a person decides to rent, buy or sell a home, one can always find help through various real estate companies or individuals who offer solutions.

Such solutions can come in the form of real estate trading services or property rental services, as well as other services necessary to complete a real estate transaction.

The real estate business is, and remains to be, a very lucrative endeavour to this day. And that seems to attract many people. Many of them are self-motivated, ambitious, self-driven, goal-oriented, enterprising individuals.

Any person can enter the real estate industry, given different career options. If you enjoy selling and doing consulting work, you can choose a real estate agent career.

With preparation and motivation, there may be no limit to what you can achieve. But with that, you need to have, if not develop, a positive frame of mind. What do you want to accomplish? What is your idea of success?

Why must real estate agents approach their real estate business the way business owners would manage their enterprise? How should they develop their creativity and brilliant mindset?

With this book, *The Brilliant Mindset of a Real Estate Agent: What it Takes to Achieve Your Goals,* you will find some insights and learn some practical approaches.

You will find case studies in which we explore two personas through the life of Lyra and Sam, who are both newly licensed real estate agents yet with very different attitudes and mindsets.

We take a closer look into their experiences and their goals. What are the approaches to their real estate undertakings?

Then, we cover topics on goals.

That would include the essence of achieving a goal. And at the same time, taking on small goals to achieve that one big goal. And why these two types of goals must link? What is the significance of each of these goals? How could goal-setters achieve their ultimate aim in their career, in business, and even in their day-to-day life?

We, further, looked at how to go about choosing one's journey. On what aspects of such a journey should one focus? Then, we touch on this very question that can seem to excite anyone: "Are You Ready for Your One Million Dollar Journey?"

In life, there are always options available in which we can choose to do. One of such options is to continue with the journey. And the other is to look at the things that we could learn (through the experience). That is like looking at the general essence of life: to live it or to learn from it. You have the power in your hands to decide on which way to go.

Being a part of this complex and challenging real estate industry, one can learn the many ropes in the real estate business.

A real estate agent can find success in their real estate business in many ways. First off, an agent can look up to some role models. Then, they can define and hone their approaches. Gradually, they go through what it takes to develop brilliant thinking. Then, learn to adapt to some changing situations.

When a real estate agent gets licensed, they can start to function in the real estate practice. That is a given. A real estate agent must have gone through a series of regulatory training requirements. They must have learned the many legal aspects that come with the real estate trading services, including other required relevant courses.

What one may not probably realize is that the real estate profession, like any other business, requires some practical self-development as part of preparation.

Real estate agents must define their purpose for entering the business. They must answer some questions, and perhaps, even one question after another. Such questions may include: "Why did I choose the real estate business, of all other business possibilities? Would my personality fit into this industry? If not, what does it take to be successful in this business?"

Real estate agents must know their strengths the same way they must acknowledge their weaknesses. They must recognize opportunities, as well as know what possible threats they are likely to encounter in their real estate business.

Real estate agents, just like entrepreneurs, must identify their available resources and how they plan to use these resources to meet their goals.

At the beginning of conducting the real estate business, real estate agents may have limited resources. Such resources may include access to finance, people, and other tools. A real estate agent must, therefore, learn to use and manage such limited resources well.

Sometimes, it is not how much you put into the table but how you execute your plan (given the resources that you have) that would matter.

The wonderful thing about becoming a real estate agent is the low barrier to entry.

However, it does not mean that the real estate business is suited to all types of people (who decide to get into the real estate industry).

Just like any other business, the real estate industry is very competitive.

More and more real estate agents get licensed and start their business year after year. So, where and how would you position yourself?

A lot has changed in how real estate marketing is done these days, given the digital evolution. And how the process of transformation boosts one's career and business.

The good news, though is, conducting a business in this digital era has signalled even more opportunities.

Real estate agents, who capitalize on the available digital media resources to create their branding, can have a better chance to establish authority and leadership in their chosen niche or market. With digital tools, such as social media, video marketing, and local marketing, real estate agents can generate leads that can result in obtaining listings and meeting new prospective buyers.

Creating and enhancing personal branding has, forever, been an essential aspect in establishing, growing, and sustaining a real estate agent's business.

As such, real estate agents must focus on creating a genuine brand with which clients can relate and connect. Clients could recognize a real estate agent's name, depending on the kind of impression real estate agents project.

Real estate agents cannot afford to be passive, with a wait-and-see mode, given the rise in competition. Agents must pursue their business and let their presence be visible in the eyes of the clients.

A real estate business is not all about location, location, location.

It is also about seeking and finding ways to learn, learn, learn.

A real estate business is not all about location, location, location.
It is also about seeking and finding ways to learn, learn, learn.

PART ONE

ENTERING THE REAL ESTATE BUSINESS

CHAPTER 1

The New Sales Person

The New Sales Person

Lyra is a newly licensed agent, who in her mid-twenties, passed the real estate licensing examination with flying colours. She looked very determined. She exhibits confidence, and anyone who sees her can tell she is very personable. In the past, Lyra was often mistaken as someone who might have appeared in TV commercials or Hollywood films. She can capture anyone's attention without much effort. And she wears fashionable clothes and dresses so well.

The truth is, Lyra has some background in fashion and clothing. She loves glamour, parties, and fun. She has had some work experience in the fashion business as a retail sales associate.

Simply put, she has worked in many fashion retail shops. That would even include some high-end fashion chains of retail stores. However, every three to six months, she would move from one company to another. It was as though she could not seem to stick around with one company, and she keeps looking for something that would satisfy her. One day, she asked herself, "Is this something that I would like to do for the rest of my life? I always feel there is something more fulfilling to do."

Until Lyra got tired of the whole thing, she thought of a career change. She thought, by doing so, maybe, she would be able to find for what, indeed, she was looking. She thought, perhaps, she needs some kind of a challenge or something to that effect. Then, she realizes working on her own could be a better choice for her, rather than working for someone else. Lyra recognizes the promise of limitless opportunities. She simply needs to explore becoming a boss for herself.

That is when she decided to venture into the real estate business as a real estate agent.

Upon passing the exam and all the requirements to become a licensed agent, Lyra made it easy to start working as a sales representative in one of the finest real estate brokerages in the city closest to where she lives. One could see how enthusiastic she was from the moment she stepped onto the office of the real estate brokerage. Lyra can easily attract attention as she appears to be with a winning personality. One would even think she does not have to attend any personality development training, as she almost displays it amazingly.

When she entered the office, the managing broker welcomed her and showed her the entire building, including the sales office (which she can use to do some paperwork or computer work).

Then, she also visited the conference room (which she could use for meetings with clients).

She also learned that she could attend weekly and monthly meetings. That is one of the ways for her to grow her knowledge in the real estate industry.

And then, the managing broker told Lyra, she could decide when and how she wants to start with her real estate sales work.

She is, after all, independent. And that she could decide on the right approach to her real estate business.

So, Lyra went to her desk and started with some computer tasks. She has her list of things to do. Her list starts with ordering business cards. Then, she visualized (and designed) some marketing flyers, which she could give out to her prospects.

She did not bother to think about creating her website at such a point. She is, after all, provided with one web page, whereby she can put some information about her, courtesy of her real estate brokerage. She thought that would do it.

Then, she further went through her list (of things to do). It occurred to her that she needed to order some real estate yard signs. She would need that for some detached homes. Then, she would need some more real estate signs for some condominium and townhouse properties.

She thought she could use such for-sale signs in case prospective home sellers would require her services. That would be: to list and sell (their properties).

After that, she thought of a marketing giveaway she could order. She thought she would need some sort of promotional materials in which her name would be visible, her contact details, and the logo of her real estate brokerage.

Would she need pens, fridge magnets, calendars, or note pads? Or all?

She was encouraged to order a bunch of these promotional giveaways, as she learned that there is a reasonable discount available through her real estate brokerage. She spent the rest of her day thinking of other things she would need to do.

The following day, she was contemplating getting herself a new car. "Maybe, just a decent sedan car will do."

She thought to herself while intently looking at the red sedan car inside the car mall.

The car salesman approached her. "Interested in that car? You know a lot of corporate women, who stop by here in our showroom, are attracted to this model."

"Really?" Lyra said. "Good, huh."

That night, inside her bedroom, Lyra can't seem to stop thinking about the red car. "Should I get it? I mean, I'm working in my very ideal career now. Well, compared to my previous job. I think I will need to upgrade now. My old car is almost five years old, and sooner or later, I will need to replace it anyway. Who knows what trouble could that old car get me into, right? Not that it is so bad, but I'm not sure if I would look presentable in the eyes of my clients. Isn't a car symbol of success? I saw my cousin Sylvie (who is also a real estate agent) driving a high-end car. And she's been getting many prospective clients, considering that she was just in her second year in the business. Was it all because of her successful image driving a brand-new car? I asked Sylvie several months ago. She said her goal was to impress her clients. True enough, she has closed some deals. That was sort of an achievement for someone who is in her first few years in the real estate business. She's right with this, I think."

Lyra got up from the bed and went on her computer to check on her finances. "I could probably get the new car through lease financing."

The next day, Lyra woke up displaying unusual excitement. She was eager to start with her plans that day.

And without delay, she went back to the car mall and purchased the car.

Days went by for several weeks, her fellow real estate agents in the real estate brokerage could see Lyra's eagerness to come to work each day, as though she was on cloud nine.

Her managing broker noticed her enthusiasm and thought that Lyra is doing amazingly, being one of the new sales agents in their real estate organization.

She would often show up in the office, including at the sales meetings.

Then, she would check on the company's listings of properties, including residential and commercial.

She would also check on other properties listed in the multiple listing service or also known as MLS. Such a service allows all real estate agents, who are members of the local real estate board, to access the members' listings.

Lyra couldn't contain her optimistic attitude as she feels she can always meet several prospects. She feels she simply has to keep doing what she was doing. And it wouldn't take that long before she could get her first sale.

Three months later, Lyra still has not closed a deal.

Despite that outcome, Lyra remained optimistic. She believes that her time to shine would happen. "One day or sooner, I would, finally, close my first sale," Lyra said, trying to convince herself.

But, after having some mixed thoughts of the situation, she extended her efforts to create a good vibe for herself.

She thought of changing something about herself - sort of inviting a more positive vibe.

She thought of improving her style of clothing. She wanted to create a new aura and to attract some positive energy.

So, one Monday afternoon, after Lyra went to her real estate brokerage office, she thought of going to the shopping mall to look for some more stylish clothes and shoes she could purchase. Lyra even thought of visiting the clothing retail store in which she used to work.

And as soon as Lyra went to the store, there was this lady who eagerly approached her. But the lady is not familiar with Lyra. "Maybe she is new here." Lyra thought to herself.

The sales lady began her sales pitch. "That blue three-piece suit would look good on you." The sales lady said and smiled at her.

"I know, I have this three-piece of clothes already," Lyra replied.

"Oh, is that right? Then you must love going here," the sales lady said.

Lyra was quiet and did not bother to reply.

The sales lady continues, "I wonder, is there anything, in particular, you are looking for? If I may ask, any function to which you need to attend?"

Lyra was silent the whole time. She scanned the store as though she was ignoring the sales lady who was so eager to serve her.

All that time, the sales lady has no idea about Lyra. That Lyra used to work in that retail store.

Despite Lyra's silence, the sales lady still looked very excited. And she continued to ask questions. "Are you looking for a specific dress or style?"

The sales lady thought that, since Lyra must be familiar with the store, given her fascination and experience in buying from their store before, she could probably help Lyra find the clothes she needed.

"You must be a valued client," the sales lady continued with her pitch until one male worker in that store recognized Lyra.

"Lyra? Is that you? Wow, you look very corporate!" said the worker.

"Hi, oh, you still work here?" Lyra replied, with some facial gestures.

"Yeah. I've been in this store, longer than anyone else has been, even you, huh. But I'm okay. You know, my wife and I need to keep up with our mortgage. So this job helps me fulfill that goal of keeping up with our payments."

"Oh, okay..." Lyra simply smiled.

"So, what's up?" The male worker asked Lyra.

"I just started working in a real estate brokerage about three months ago. You know, my dream job."

"Oh, I have no idea you're in the real estate business now. Big time, huh!"

Lyra didn't know how to properly reply to that comment, as that was the first time someone had told her about that remark, "big time!"

She thought to herself, *Is this the image someone sees on people working on real estate? Wow, that must be something. People look up to you?*

"Ah yeah... I got so lucky. I passed the exam quite easily. And you know..." Lyra continued bragging about her experience and did not think about the two people in front of her, who were just observing.

"By the way, could I still get a discount here? You know, being a former employee," Lyra asked.

"That's not my department, though," the male worker said. "Ask Bev."

"Who's Bev? The new manager?"

"Not exactly. She is the new manager trainee. There she is, in front of you," the male worker was pointing to the sales lady Lyra was talking to earlier.

"Sorry, you no longer work here. No more privileges," the sales lady replied.

"What? Okay, fine. I'll just go to the other store. Thanks, anyway."

* * *

A LOOK INTO THE SITUATION

Looking at the earlier scenario, what do you think Lyra could have done differently now that she is a real estate agent, although she used to work as a retail store associate?

Was Lyra emotional? Was she offended when she thought that she could not get a discount? Was that the reason she decided to leave, and she would go to the other store?

What seems to be the impression of the people present at the time towards Lyra?

Did Lyra underestimate the sales lady?

Would the situation be different had Lyra been more friendly and open to conversation?

What opportunities did Lyra miss out on when a former male co-worker approached her (who later told her that he needed to keep the job at the retail store)?

Was Lyra not paying attention when his former co-worker mentioned why the job is necessary for him and his wife? That they have to meet their mortgage payments?

Did it not occur to Lyra that the male co-worker and the wife could plan to move to another property at some point? Or they might plan to sell their property to ease up the burden of mortgage payments? Did not Lyra think of listening to the male co-worker and dig a little deeper and see how she could help, just in case?

Was Lyra carried away by the compliment? That she looks as though she is 'big time' now? That she even mentioned she's finally doing her dream job?

Did it not occur to Lyra that she could offend the former male co-worker? That was when she said, "You still work here?" Was not Lyra paying attention to the male co-worker's story that she did not seem to connect appropriately?

Was Lyra doing a favour to herself when she thought dressing up differently and buying more stylish clothes could change her atmosphere? And that she could attract good energy?

How was Lyra taking the outcome from what she has been doing? And that after three months of working as a real estate agent, she still has not closed a deal?

What was Lyra's mindset? Was her attitude toward being optimistic helping her to keep up with her belief? That her time to shine will come?

What could Lyra have done differently during her first three months in the real estate brokerage?

Was Lyra in a good environment, in which everybody looks at her as though she's doing fine? Did Lyra ever open up and ask for specific advice or guidance from her managing broker?

Was Lyra practical when she appears as though she was doing all right in the eyes of her peers?

Given Lyra's reasons that she needs to be presentable, was it a good move for Lyra to purchase a new car? Was it all right that Lyra looks up to her real estate agent cousin, Sylvie, whose goal was to impress clients, and so having a high-end car is inevitable, or so, she thought?

On Lyra's first day at the real estate brokerage office, she wanted to focus on some administrative, and perhaps, some marketing tasks. Lyra has outlined several tasks to execute on that day. She believes that such tasks are a must-do set of tasks. Was Lyra practical for including those tasks in her list? Are those a good set of tasks to execute during your first day of work?

If you were in her shoes, how would you approach your first day at work? What would you do differently?

Was Lyra's objective to get into the real estate business a good reason to become a real estate agent?

If you are Lyra, would you still pursue the career of a real estate agent despite having not a single sale in three months? How do you think one could survive, given that situation? Should Lyra already stop to pursue her real estate career?

What are Lyra's admirable characteristics? How about her strengths? What are her weaknesses? What are Lyra's good decisions and bad decisions? Has Lyra seen the threats in the real estate industry before getting into the real estate business?

What opportunities could you see that Lyra might have missed? How should Lyra position her frame of mind?

CHAPTER 2

A Point of Discovery

A Point of Discovery

A real estate agent must reflect upon the likely scenarios in the life and embodiment of a real estate agent.

What does being in real estate mean to you? Why do you want to zone into the world of a real estate agent?

The moment you decide to enter the real estate business, as a real estate agent, you must ask a series of questions relevant to your situation. Take the case of Lyra's situation. Such questions could help you prepare before and during the time you are pursuing your real estate profession.

You see, asking the right questions is never easy. You will have to assess every point in a situation. At first, thinking of what to ask, how to ask, when to ask, where to ask, and why to ask can be overwhelming. But as you get used to that essential task of discovery, you would, eventually, be able to acquire a good set of skills.

Asking a question is a skill. More so, finding the right approach to seeking answers.

When you work with a client, you must demonstrate your ability to understand your client's situation. For the most part, you must exercise your listening skill. By doing that, you allow your client to express their thoughts. What is their goal? You must be able to discover their motivation and reasons for buying or selling a home. Such a point of discovery would begin by asking the right questions at the right time.

As a real estate agent, you must devote some thinking time to allow the process to set into your inner system.

You can gradually develop your style. You will get to learn more about yourself and your strengths. And you would know what to do in some cases with which you may not be familiar. What would you do when you face a situation that challenges your weakness and limitation?

How should you position your frame of mind?

* * *

WHAT'S YOUR FRAME OF MIND?

Big goals. Small goals. Have you thought about your goals? For your first year in real estate? Perhaps, you were thinking of some dollar numbers?

In setting goals, do you know your reasons for doing so? Where would you start? Would you start big? Or would you start small?

Some would probably say, start small. It is something easy to do. It is something easy to achieve, right? And it is easier to feel confident that you could do it.

In reality, setting small goals is very common to most people.

In most cases, people can accomplish things daily by setting the usual things to do. And things would become like second nature. It becomes automatic. And voila, you get your way. There is your accomplished goal. You could do things.

You would get what you had thought was even impossible with which to begin.

Take, for instance, when you are an employee of a company. You are assigned tasks to do. There are expectations from you as an employee.

You could probably get other assignments or other responsibilities. That would depend on the department under which you work. There might be some instances when responsibilities could be new to you. Therefore, you might have a new set of tasks. In effect, you can probably regard these new tasks as a challenge to you.

You will find that, since these new tasks do not have the same procedure as the other things in your previous routine, you will probably seek a better approach to accomplishing your new goals much faster.

In that way, you can impress your bosses or your immediate supervisor. And you could be up for promotion. And even better, you could receive some kind of performance bonus. That would reward you for the job well executed.

As new days, weeks, months pass, you will realize you are getting better and better with the job. And you will be accustomed to doing it, as it has now become a routine to you. It's like you breathe with it, in and out. You could explore the process with ease, and you find it convenient to communicate with others.

You are one of those employees of which the company can be proud. The company has reached its goals. You made that happen.

GOAL AS AN EMPLOYEE

The small goals as an employee that you have been trying to accomplish are, in essence, part of the big goals the company has set for its business.

In reality, the company is accomplishing the vision it has originally stated for its business organization.

The company must set the plans. The company leaders, such as the directors and managers of the company, must strategically assign small goals and tasks to their downline.

That would include various departments such as the marketing, sales, customer service, production, accounting, and finance departments that make up the whole organization.

Each of those employees, who work in their respective departments, is assigned a set of small tasks and goals. The upper management would monitor their subordinates. The company managers must see the various members in their organization. They must assess their workers' performance. They must ask the right questions. Are they keeping up with their assigned small goals? And whether they are contributing to the bigger goals or the overall goals of the business.

Where are we going with that scenario? That could tell us that every part of the organization is essential. And that every person has a role to play. Every small part of the organization would help make the whole system going.

In other words, smaller goals make up the bigger goal.

Every employee is part of the bigger picture of the business organization.

The company leaders, such as the upper managers and directors, must think of the direction and activities their business must undertake. They must think of the strategies they must employ and execute to achieve their bigger goals.

That would mean achieving an impressive revenue with which all stakeholders would be happy.

GOAL AS A REAL ESTATE AGENT

Now, as a real estate agent, how do you think that you start with your goal? Do you think of yourself as an employee?

Isn't that as a real estate agent, even though you are part of a real estate brokerage, you are working independently?

You are, by virtue, a self-employed person.

You are no longer an employee who could expect a regular salary (or who could receive an employee's compensation).

You would not think of yourself the way an employed person in a business organization would. You would not do employee's tasks this time. You are working for yourself.

You will now embark on a different journey.

You will now be running an independent venture. This time, you will be your boss.

You will be your manager. How would you go about setting goals now that you are working for yourself? And the income you will earn would depend on how you look at your vision for your venture.

At this point, your brilliance as a real estate agent will begin, depending on how you set your frame of mind.

Would you aim more and higher? Would you approach your goal as a real estate agent the way a business owner would approach entrepreneurship? Or how large businesses would look at their bigger goals?

If you aim higher, then you are setting yourself up to achieving bigger goals.

In essence, you are no longer just part of a whole.

You will be the main goal-setter of that big goal. You are the prime mover and strategist, in which you will have to look at the whole picture. And see how you will go about accomplishing small goals that could contribute to reaching the bigger goal.

Setting 'big goals' do not necessarily mean you aim for the highest amount of money. Unless, of course, that is your only goal in life. Is it? For sure, there are other vital aspects in your life.

"Wait, money should be the goal in real estate, right? That is why I went into this business!"

Many real estate agents would say they get into the real estate business because of the unlimited earning potential.

While it is true that money is a great motivation to get into the real estate business, it is not the 'be all and end all' for every real estate agent. If it is, why do many real estate agents leave the industry in their first year of operation, if not much earlier?

Should money be the focus? Are there other factors that could serve as a motivation to get into this business of real estate?

Look at the case of Lyra in the beginning chapter of this book. She had thought of entering the real estate business when she got tired of her job in the retail industry. She got bored in her routine. She wants to pursue a fulfilling career. And by becoming a real estate agent, she thought she could be on her way to reaching her goals. That is by becoming her boss.

The problem is, did she even set her goals? Did she look at a longer time horizon? Also, since she did not make a single sale in the first three months, what do you think should she do? Should she give up already at such a point? Or could she find a better way to approach her real estate business?

Yes, the idea is to aim higher. But, we should look at that idea whereby we set the big goals as the way to go. That is to enjoy the journey in life.

Look at the word journey.

YOUR JOURNEY AND YOUR GOALS

Journey lets you explore the beauty and wonder in each of the challenges that may come your way. What comes with our life's journey would not be pure exciting experiences. One could expect challenges. One could be up for some difficulties, depending on how one has prepared before getting into this business.

Many people could get disappointed with the whole situation. Many people tend to get discouraged in the early stages of their journey. Sometimes, people get one distraction, then, there they are, they could be thinking of giving up.

Not necessarily giving up on the big goals, I suppose.

The idea of money is probably still there, or whatever goals you might have thought about, even before getting into this industry.

In many cases, people are giving up on the journey, not on the goals.

However, if you give up on the journey itself, where could you find yourself direction-wise? How do you expect to get to your destination? Isn't the end of the tunnel where you could find your big goals?

One may come and go into any other industry. You may change your career or business.

There is something you might notice, though. Your big goals could still be there. Perhaps, relatively, the same. If not, maybe, somewhat altered.

You know for yourself what you wanted to achieve. You know by heart that very goal. Whatever that might be, you know it in your inner soul, deep within you.

Goals can be a reflection of your inner self. They could direct you to what you want to achieve in your life.

You may experience thinking about it daily. Or you may dream about it some years from now. But it is within you. You just have to listen to yourself. Take some time to reflect upon your inner thoughts.

It reflects your lifestyle. It reflects how other people can influence your day-to-day decisions and actions. People want to achieve something. It is human nature to want to accomplish something you have been longing, all your life.

Our experiences could tell us or direct us to that point of many possibilities. And that may even lead us to change our circumstances.

The problem, though, is that some people do not realize what they want in life. "What do I want for myself? For my family? For other people? How do I want to take part in sharing the blessings that I receive?"

Becoming a real estate professional can almost equate to the steps to becoming wealthy. There is truth to that. There is what we call 'unlimited income potential' in real estate.

You can be a millionaire.

Real estate is an industry whereby you could witness, see, or hear many successful stories. You could see many successful real estate agents who excel in their respective areas of operation.

Isn't that if there is something you can easily prove, people can instantly believe?

Some people might even believe (in stories) without knowing the underlying factors behind such stories.

Many factors contribute to achieving success. It is not a one-time activity of which one could think. Then, you believe you can be on your way to reaching that level of success.

Consistency is key to your approach, as adaptability is essential to dealing with change.

There is your one big goal. Yes, we should aim for that big goal.

In looking at your big goal, you could set the whole picture of your journey.

At first, it could just be a product of imagination. You are painting that mental picture in your head. You believe that, at some point, you will accomplish that. It takes the right thinking. It takes setting the right frame of mind.

Take, for instance, the scenario whereby many first-time homebuyers have been dreaming of owning their own home. Their big goal is to be able to purchase a property they could call their own.

Several factors could contribute to that goal. Yet, the point is, setting that big goal, painting the mental picture in one's mind, would inspire one to keep going in their daily life. They will enjoy the journey each day. They are motivated to achieve that big goal. They will prepare for it.

They will take baby steps. And these baby steps are their small goals.

Small goals are essentials to get to their big goals. Therefore, first-time buyers will need to set their small goals.

They will save up for the required down payment.

They will research what it takes to qualify for financing.

They will consult with professionals.

They will work on improving their credit.

They can be willing to change their lifestyle to accomplish their savings goals. They will set their time frame.

They will talk to licensed real estate professionals, including real estate agents, mortgage brokers, lending officers, home inspectors, appraisers, lawyers, and other professionals.

They will even talk to their neighbours, relatives, or other people they know who have bought their own homes.

Looking at the above steps, one can conclude that it takes some preparation to get to the end of the road. That is the one big goal.

Setting your one big goal can start by setting or even re-setting your frame of mind.

What is your frame of mind?

A real estate agent must know where to start and where to go. Hence, where do you focus your thinking?

A real estate agent must think the way entrepreneurs would think about their business.

They must think of themselves as a leading figure in their enterprise.

"What do I want for my business? What is the goal or the big goal? What are the necessary steps to accomplish that big goal? What would be my small goals? What are my resources? How do I prepare for my venture? How do I go about my journey?"

CHAPTER 3

A One Million Dollar Journey

A One Million Dollar Journey

Sam is a real estate agent in the real estate brokerage where Lyra works. Unlike Lyra (who, at that point, is in her third month in the company), Sam is only in his first week.

Sam is ambitious and determined to succeed. He is very enthusiastic and confident. He knows his one big goal. That is to earn his first million dollars. Sam's enthusiasm amazes everyone.

"Wow, that is very inspiring! Sam knows what he wants, eh!" says the managing broker, who was discussing a topic on setting goals.

One fellow agent named Mark, who was with the company for almost three years, asked Sam politely, "How do you plan to reach your first million?"

Sam said, "Hmmm... interesting question! But I think I know the answer."

Every real estate agent in the conference room has heard the discussion. And they were all eager to hear Sam's response.

Sam replied, "That is easy! I just need to find one good listing with a value of twenty million dollars. And assuming that I can have the client list the property at five percent commission for the listing agent, that should give me my first million earnings!"

"That's incredible!" Mark said as he applauded Sam. Some other agents also followed Mark's gesture and made louder applause.

Then, Mark continued with his remark toward Sam. "You must know a lot of wealthy people. Well, good luck to you on your goal, Sam!"

After two months of searching and prospecting, Sam finally found a client with a house to sell. The property is worth about twenty million dollars. Sam could not contain his excitement. "Wow, wow, and wow! I could not believe this! It is happening, huh!"

His managing broker was so happy with the listing. He even gave Sam some pointers on how to market the property, given it was Sam's first listing.

Sam is a fast learner. He researches how to market an upscale property as sophisticated as this listing. He contacted a professional photographer to capture beautiful images of the property. He even consulted a home stager that could help him with the decoration and staging of the property. Then, he decided to do a video to showcase different areas of the home.

Next, he made some digital and print brochures.

Sam decided to spend on advertising. After all, he thought he could establish his presence better in that way. His name would be visible in advertising materials, including digital channels.

One can see, Sam is very creative. Many of his fellow real estate agents are impressed. That is the way Sam approaches his spending. It would show that Sam has financial resources to cover the marketing and advertising costs of his listing.

Sam and his wife recently got a line of credit. But that was secured through their residential property. His wife was aware of

Sam's real estate marketing activities and agreed for Sam to use the equity in their home.

With all hopes up, Sam is indeed excited with his very first property listing.

He would update his clients (sellers) with his marketing activities.

He would hold open houses almost every weekend. He would invite other real estate agents, especially buyers' agents, to bring in their clients.

Sam also made sure that the buyer's agent would be well-compensated. That is as per his agreement with his client (or the seller).

Sam was focused on this property. Therefore, he decided not to get distracted by other activities. That would include prospecting for other possible property listings.

Sam was doing everything he could for his client's property. He decided to spend longer hours showing the home. On several showings, Sam would often go home late at night, as some possible buyers are only available on certain nights.

His wife understood Sam's reasons. She was very supportive of Sam, especially that she sees Sam's hard work.

Besides, his wife finds the goal of reaching one million dollars very motivating. And so, they decided to go all in.

Sam spent more and more on advertising, with the hope that the right buyer will come along.

Truth be told, after some six months of waiting, an offer came in. Sam presented the offer to his client. However, the offer is too low, way below his seller's asking price. Sam's client was not happy. Therefore, the offer did not push through.

Sam, along with his wife, was devastated. His wife asked him, "Sam, is that how hard to find a good buyer for that kind of listing? I thought things would be easy?"

Sam replied to his wife, "I did not know it would be this hard. The listing is there. You've seen the property, right? It's like half of the transaction is there. I just need to find the right buyer who could afford the price."

Sam's wife expressed some not-so-good facial gestures, showing disappointment in the whole situation. "So, what now, Sam? If you don't close a deal in the next few months, we would be broke. We almost maxed out our credit limit. And I don't know how we would be able to pay our mortgage, plus the money we owe from the line of credit. Think about that, Sam."

After about nine months, the listing remains open. A handful, prospective buyers showed up on the last scheduled open house.

That worries Sam to a great extent. He was thinking about his wife, his debts, and his relationship with his client. He also worries this can end his career. Sam is almost on the verge of going broke.

And the worst outcome, his marriage could suffer tremendously. And if Sam does not do the appropriate action, based on his current situation, he could lose so much of his net worth, given that their home has two mortgages in it.

And the possibility that he has to deal with a much bigger problem, his marriage.

Finally, Sam asked, "Where have I gone wrong?"

PART TWO

ACHIEVING A BRILLIANT MINDSET

CHAPTER 4

Achieving a Smart Mindset

Achieving a Smart Mindset

In the scenario from the previous chapter, what do you think Sam could have done in his chosen journey?

Did Sam have a good mindset to begin his real estate journey as an agent?

How did his big goal of one million dollars move him to direct his steps?

Wasn't he stuck on that single idea?

What do you think about Sam's frame of mind when he thought that his only way of reaching his millions is through one listing of twenty million dollars worth of property? Wasn't he focused on that one thing alone? Could he have thought of other small goals until he could get to his 'big goal' of one million dollars?

To dream big is not at all bad.

But, what made Sam's story complicated?

To think of 'big goals' is not what makes the whole story complex. It is about thinking of the ways to go about that goal that can make or break the entirety of it.

To strive to achieve a brilliant mindset would equate to trying to achieve different approaches to every setback. That is when the hypothetical question an entrepreneurial person might need to ask: "What if?"

Preparation is about knowing what to do in case something does not end up the way to which you would want.

Preparation is about knowing the risks that may come with each of the decisions you make.

Preparation is about learning to be level-headed upon the whole journey into which you would embark.

In life, there are always options available in which we could choose to do. First of all, you could decide to continue with your journey. And the next, you could look at the things that you could learn through some experience.

It is like looking at the general essence of life: to live it or to learn from it. You have the power in your hands to decide on which way to go.

How should one plan to start with a one million dollar journey? You see, that question about achieving one million dollars is an example of a big goal.

Looking at that, you could think of several small goals in which you could achieve, and that would lead to getting to that same big goal.

You could break it down to make it achievable.

When you think of your small goals, you will need to qualify whether you are making sense with the steps that you would do.

Have you heard about the acronym SMART?

Some people may be familiar with the said acronym when it comes to goal-setting.

It stands for specific, measurable, attainable, reasonable or realistic, and time-based.

To learn to master the art of creating goals would be an essential aspect in establishing and developing a brilliant mindset.

To learn to master the art of creating goals would be an essential aspect in establishing and developing a brilliant mindset.

It takes some practice to enhance the skills in setting, planning, and executing your goal. There are times that you may need to adjust, depending on the situation.

But, you have to be committed and motivated to essentially look at all the vital components to achieve the goal.

In my book, *Savings Mix: How to Manage Money and Achieve Savings and Goals,* I touched on the topic of creating goals, the smart way.

When we think of goal-setting, we would need to identify the goal first and foremost. That means we are setting a target.

For example, when someone says, "I want to travel to Europe." That statement is a very general goal, which may or may not happen.

However, when a person says, "I want to travel to Europe next year with a budget of approximately ten thousand dollars (10K), which means I will need to do some planning at home. I will need to set aside some funds equivalent to one hundred ninety-three dollars ($193) every week for fifty-two weeks starting next week, which might necessitate giving up going to fancy restaurants or adjusting my weekly budget. I will need to do that so I can achieve my goal to travel to Europe next year." Then, we could tell that person refers to a defined goal.

Such a 'defined goal' would be the first step to creating a 'smart' mindset.

You might have noticed that the 'defined goal' seemed to have answered the vital questions. Such questions begin with 'W' (who, what, why, where, when, which).

Who will set the goal? And who will execute the plan? In that scenario, it will be "I" or the person who created the goal.

Then, here comes the 'what' question that goes: *What activity or step do I need to do to accomplish my goal?*

"I need to set aside some funds equivalent to one hundred ninety-three dollars ($193)."

In effect, that response is equivalent to creating a small goal that would lead to that big goal.

Additional steps may be necessary. That would somehow depend on how you are doing so far.

Why am I doing this?

"So that I could achieve my goal to travel to Europe next year."

Where? Where do I start with my plan?

"I will need to do some planning at home."

When? And how often should I set aside such funds?

"Every week for fifty-two weeks, starting next week."

Which of the many things I do will I have to give up or sacrifice?

"Giving up going to fancy restaurants or adjusting my weekly budget."

You see, having a 'smart' mindset is like going through a process. That requires some thinking time. And to be able to plan with utmost care and put it into realization.

Setting a goal, preparing the plan, and executing according to the set of approaches make up the whole journey.

A real estate agent must think, plan, and execute strategies with a goal-oriented mindset.

Now, the steps are not complete yet.

There are still more questions to ask.

"How do I know I am getting there?" This question should refer to the goal being measurable (or the M in the SMART acronym).

"Am I able to consistently put the one hundred ninety-three dollars ($193) every week? If not, I may need to adjust. That could mean I would need to add twice the amount in the next two weeks."

With time being a component of the plan, it is imperative to specify a target day or week, or month.

In this way, you are creating a schedule on which you can work with ease. You may have to adjust or rework if and when to which you need.

The questions that follow would correspond to the rest of the acronym.

"Is my goal attainable?"

"Is it realistic?"

"Is it time-based?"

You would know the answers to the said questions if, after some time, you could still keep up with your plan.

If the plan to reach the goal does not seem attainable or realistic, or you are falling behind, at such a point, you can try to adjust.

Find other means, given your current situation.

If your goal is the ten thousand dollars (10K) amount, and after breaking it down to smaller goals, you could end up, perhaps, with two thousand five hundred dollars ($2500) every three months, four times a year.

You could adjust the plan and look at the six months time horizon instead. Let's say you can plan for three thousand dollars ($3000) for twenty-six weeks of setting aside one hundred sixteen dollars ($116) every week.

Now, since you are doing the plan, you would know for a fact where you are at, given your situation and your view of your goals.

You may not achieve the goal in itself, let's say in a year, but you could perhaps get it, say a year and a half after.

At least, that one big goal that you have had could serve as a driving force to get to where you are now.

Remember, the plan that you are making is not there that serves to be an 'absolute' plan.

It is there to guide you with your journey.

It is like a map that could tell you the road to take. So, you could arrive at your planned destination.

At some point or in the future, you may need to go on an unrecognizable route. A route through which you would think would seem impossible to pass. You may need to take a detour. Or do some kind of re-calibrating, looking at a compass until you could find your direction back to your desired destination.

But at the end of the day, you will reach your destination point. There may be some delays, but that would be part of the whole journey, wouldn't it?

We are in this life to unfold the right journey that we will take. And with it, we find some joys and thrills instead of getting consumed with the setback.

Now, as a real estate agent, your role is to plan for your journey.

Think of your goals to let you explore various approaches. And that will take you to the end station of your journey.

That is your final goal.

But then, some would stop on certain stations. Or in most cases, we look through our small goals. People decide on it. No one tells them how far they should go. No one would decide for them except themselves.

Some may already be satisfied at such a point. And decide to stop there.

They have realized their goal. It may be one goal, not so fancy, nothing grand. And that may mean reaching a short trip or a quick destination. That is an experience in itself.

However, as a real estate agent, how far do you think you could go?

As a real estate agent, there can be a long journey ahead for you, which could take you to several stops.

And that would depend on how, as a real estate agent, you would look at the whole journey.

Some people could get tired before even reaching some more stops. And then, they could decide to leave at the nearest point.

Many new real estate agents could go through almost the same experience. So, it is imperative to know yourself closely.

Where are you at this point?

Are you enjoying the ride?

Some people would decide to continue to travel through some small stops. They would not mind passing through more stations.

With every point of stop, some people would view the experience as a learning opportunity.

Real estate agents, who think that way, are likely to set and develop their 'right frame of mind'. Real estate agents can indeed find their way to achieve their 'smart' mindset.

CHAPTER 5

Achieving an Entrepreneurial Mindset

Achieving an Entrepreneurial Mindset

Real estate agents must embrace the idea of having an entrepreneurial mindset.

Before one decides to pursue entrepreneurship, or in the case of a real estate agent, one is encouraged to identify what makes up being entrepreneurial.

What characteristics should an entrepreneurial real estate agent possess? How should one define success?

Many would point success to the ability of a person to possess skills, such as management skills, technical skills, and perhaps, some kind of specialized skills.

And many people would think that such skills and knowledge would be what they would need to carry out the duties (of managing a real estate business).

And they hope they will achieve their intended results.

But then, we wonder, how come many entrepreneurs, or in this case, real estate agents, leave the industry so early? While some successful entrepreneurial agents are thriving.

What seems to be the reason? Or what should one possess to survive and keep on with their venture?

What sets an entrepreneurial real estate agent apart from the crowd?

In my other book, *Micro Enterprise Marketing: How to Start, Promote and Grow Your Micro Business in the Digital Age*, I have touched on the idea of having an entrepreneurial mindset.

In a nutshell, having an entrepreneurial mindset is integral in achieving success.

Many people attempt to define entrepreneurial success.

Yet, you would end up hearing several answers. And why is that?

That is because success could mean different things to different people. We all have different goals. We identify our big goals. And from there, we set our small goals.

Some people may already be satisfied at some level. Others could keep pushing to the next level until they could maximize their potential. As a real estate agent, where do you intend to be?

What should an entrepreneur or real estate agent do to achieve that thing called 'entrepreneurial mindset'?

Well, a business or an entrepreneur can try different approaches.

However, could you compare a micro-business venture such as a real estate agent business to a medium-to-large business?

If you look at large business organizations, you would see a formal structure in their business operation.

On the other hand, entrepreneurs have unique ways to deal with their problems.

First of all, entrepreneurs are, in most cases, the only ones to mainly operate their enterprise.

Entrepreneurs may work with one or two employees. They could hire their assistants or sub-contractors. But they are the thinkers and enablers of their decisions. They would come up with solutions to their business problems.

Entrepreneurs or real estate agents may create their structure. They can be simple yet creative with their business operation. They can be a little loose. They can allow space for improvement. They can be fluid and adaptive.

They could think of several approaches to their problem without waiting for some people to tell them what to do.

While any business person can deal with the technical aspect of an enterprise, or any venture, at that, like having unique offerings or enhancing tailored services, in most cases, it is not enough, as there are still many other aspects in the business.

You may know the ins and outs in the industry in which you operate. But if you do not possess the right frame of mind to tackle one problem after another, you may not withstand the challenges that may come your way.

A person must find whatever it takes to be truly entrepreneurial. You must keep going despite having limited resources.

You must prepare yourself to think through several strategies and tactics. The point is to survive with the business endeavour despite the limited resources.

A person with an entrepreneurial mindset must think beyond the ordinary situation. After all, entrepreneurs work on the process with creative approaches.

It is like going through the processes by thinking outside the box. There is no single 'absolute' solution to a problem. You must embrace the power that goes with critical thinking.

That is as though you play a chess game. You can find better ways to move.

You could go forward, move backward, or sideways. You could even move in a diagonal position. If you think that would be a wiser move.

You do not remain where you are.

You will have to keep finding a way to move up.

You move just how a real estate agent in you must think.

You go on just how you must enjoy the journey that you are in right now.

You will have to keep going until you reach your destination.

And then, you would be ready to ask the question, "Where am I going next?"

CHAPTER 6

Achieving a Creative Mindset

Achieving a Creative Mindset

Having a creative mindset almost overlaps with the concept of having an entrepreneurial mindset.

A real estate agent, to be truly entrepreneurial, must learn to think of various strategies and tactics to keep growing.

That means a real estate agent must have that critical thinking ability. You must positively think beyond the obvious.

Having a creative mindset means you can be very imaginative and innovative with coming up with practical solutions.

One must be resourceful. A person must match such resources with the right tools and tactics. That would help maintain, if not enhance, the image you have built or have started to create.

Assess which of the creative tools that you have identified make the most sense in terms of output. What would be the impact of each of the tools that you have selected to use? How do these tools make up the overall marketing plan?

There are several ways in which a real estate agent can be creative.

However, some agents may find creativity a challenge. Some real estate agents may have a very different (or radical) background. Some of the agents may not think of varied approaches. Some may be uneasy in researching some practical tools.

If you find that is not natural to you, you may seek help. There are different ways you can approach the whole process, yet you can arrive at the same goal.

Remember, being a real estate agent is thinking like an entrepreneur. You must know your goals. You must know the means to achieve such goals. You must identify the steps to get there. You must identify available resources. And match such resources with your needs as a real estate agent.

In most cases, entrepreneurs know their strengths and weaknesses. Entrepreneurs tap into their strengths to remain focused and to keep things going. In some areas where they are not doing well, they could find help.

If real estate agents are to function as an entrepreneur, they must think of themselves the way business owners would think. Therefore, an entrepreneurial real estate agent must somehow work like how a chief officer (or CEO) in an organization would function. A CEO creates a plan to lead the company. A CEO would outline the necessary steps (to execute such a plan). There may be parts in the plan whereby other functions would be essential to execute. Not all these functions will have to be done by the CEO himself.

A CEO defines the job that will have to be fulfilled, then find people to deliver the required tasks. In the same way, real estate agents must think of themselves just how a CEO would manage the business operation. They must outline the steps necessary to fulfill the tasks required. And if it is something outside their strengths and skills, they would seek help.

That means, as real estate agents who may require something that is beyond their expertise, they can tap into their available resources.

Real estate agents have three resources in their hands and in which they can utilize. These resources pertain to time, money, and people.

You will need time to assess and look into this aspect of creativity. That would mean finding a variety of ways to solve a problem. You will need to look into your financial resources. To be creative means you may need to embrace the idea of practicality. At that point, the problem is seeking and finding support. That could help you on those tasks you could not do yourself.

Along the way, you may come up with some ideas. Or, if you learned some new things, you may find yourself asking some questions.

"How will these tools help my real estate business in achieving my goals down the road?"

"Would these tools require expertise from certain people who can help me fulfill my objectives?"

"Would the cost to utilize these tools be within my set budget?"

"How do I go about this?"

You can begin to survey the many digital tools available. You may find tools that other real estate professionals are using.

Then, find the time to assess each of these tools. You may include in your marketing plan some of these tools.

Now, just because you have no background or experience in using some of these tools would not mean you would not want to learn about its features and benefits.

You can hire a specialist or a marketing assistant. You may also consider some remote help, like, a virtual assistant or consultant.

You can ask them about these marketing tools.

How are such tools executed?

And how could these tools practically help you?

What creative strategy would be effective in your marketing approach?

Most of the digital tools available today have been beneficial to many businesses, depending on the objectives they are trying to accomplish.

Know what you could expect.

Know the purpose of why you are using a particular tool.

What are your objectives?

WHAT ARE YOUR OBJECTIVES?

Would the purpose be to generate leads?

Would you need to add new contacts to your prospective client list? You can then turn such leads to become your active clients or home buyers. Or you can obtain new listings from your database of prospective home sellers.

Would the purpose be to establish your brand?

As a new real estate agent, branding is imperative. You may, perhaps, try to tap into a competitive market. Such a market might have been saturated (by other real estate agents). Some of the real estate agents are well-established in their niche.

You must understand the 'ins and outs' of your chosen market.

You must be familiar with your competitors. You must learn about the many aspects of your competition. That would help you decide on your approach before entering your target niche. Ultimately, you must create a brand that would work for your real estate business. And that can establish recall of your name with ease.

Is it to maintain or improve on your current standing in your niche?

You may be well-known, but remember, there are always new players getting into the picture. Some newer real estate agents can be more proactive in their marketing activities, and the more others become visible, the more you will have to think of improving your position in your niche.

With many new real estate agents entering the real estate market, we can expect competition to grow stronger.

Where would you position your real estate business at such a point?

Is your brand still recognizable?

And does it remain the 'go-to' brand name when it comes to serving your niche?

Remember, there's always that possibility that clients can change their preferences over time.

Change is imminent. And your key is connecting and communicating through the right channel.

Would the purpose be to educate your clients?

Or, would the objective be to become a thought leader or authority in your niche?

Becoming an authority or expert takes some time. You will need to be creative and decide on how you want to be viewed by your niche. What impression do you want to create? Would you be in the real estate industry for the long haul?

> *Becoming an authority or expert takes some time.*
> *You will need to be creative and decide on how you want*
> *to be viewed by your niche. What impression do you*
> *want to create?*

The advantage of being a real estate authority is that, even in the future, should you decide to change direction in your business or career, you carry that image with you.

Let's say, at some point, you graduate from being a sales agent to becoming the managing broker or owner of your own real estate company and even other sorts of business. That image that you have created today goes with you wherever you decide to go.

Your brand could be lasting. It is like there is that mark that has been embossed on you that people know you to be such an industry expert.

Deciding to be an expert is thinking of the right image you want to project. Like if you are a buyer's agent, you might want to become the agent for first-time buyers who are starting to build a family.

Or, if you would like to focus on getting real estate listings, you, probably, would like to create a brand that you are great at helping home sellers in your target area.

PART THREE

THE REAL ESTATE PROFESSION

CHAPTER 7

The Real Estate Environment

The Real Estate Environment

Being in the real estate business can put anyone into such a challenging environment. Real estate is challenging enough for home sellers. But, it is more difficult and complex for homebuyers, especially first-time homebuyers. What does that tell you about the people who work in the industry? It tells us that everyone must perform the roles the way one should know where to position oneself.

Are you a new real estate agent? Or, do you have some years of experience in this business? And yet, you still find the world of real estate too complex.

True enough, real estate is complex. When you deal with such large amounts of transactions, considering the dollar value, such as buying or selling of properties, it is a given that you deal with a complex process. You even involve many professionals to complete the transaction, not to mention the two parties, the buyer and the seller.

A real estate agent, or to be more specific, a homebuyer's agent, is instrumental for introducing a property or list of properties to home buyers.

Then, a home seller agent is in charge of marketing and selling the home or property, on behalf of the seller, at the highest possible amount or value.

On the other hand, a bank, a financial company, a lender, and mortgage brokers are the very heart of the financial aspect of the real estate transaction. Unless, of course, one is buying using an all-cash payment. But that is very rare. Most real estate transactions in Canada and the USA are carried out through some form of financing. And that would be possible with the help of banks and lenders.

Therefore, a real estate agent has to be familiar and knowledgeable with the whole process. A buyer agent must be able to pre-qualify, and if possible, be able to guide the buyer to obtain a pre-approval from the bank and lender. That is to ensure that the buyers are qualified before viewing a set of properties and even before offering a deal on the property they intend to buy.

Then, there's the home inspection part. That could be critical to the whole transaction. A home inspection or a professional home inspection report can spell the difference. That can make or even break a deal. Such an inspection outcome can form part of the conditions in the purchase and sale contract. The buyer must be satisfied with the physical condition of the property before deciding to go ahead with the transaction.

As a professional real estate agent, you must be familiar with the nature of the deal. You should be knowledgeable about the legal aspects of each transaction. And in case of doubt or confusion, have your client contact a lawyer to look into and go over the transaction details.

Real estate agents must advise their clients to seek independent legal advice before entering and completing any agreements.

In doing so, real estate agents are doing their professional duties. That would also relieve them from any legal responsibility in which only lawyers must carry out.

Lawyers have their respective duties and obligations, different from real estate agents.

So, a real estate agent must never assume that duty to perform the part in which a lawyer should do. And that also applies to all other real estate professionals in the industry.

You would not function as if you know the whole thing about a property you are buying or selling on behalf of your clients.

Let home inspectors do their part and execute their duty.

In the same way, you would not assume all other duties and roles.

That would include the duties of an appraiser, mortgage broker, electrician, and plumber (and other relevant, professional real estate duties one could think about). Unless, you are licensed and authorized to do so and you are prepared to assume any liabilities.

It is always safe to focus on your role as a real estate agent for your client.

What you could do is provide a list of professionals and companies. The list could serve as a resource tool. You could put the list on your website. Or you may want to send the list to your clients via email.

Many clients would appreciate it, and they can freely decide on whom to hire. They can browse your list of mortgage brokers, home inspectors, appraisers, and lawyers. Your list may also include other professionals such as a home stager, videographer, and real estate photographer.

It would be better not to recommend specific names or companies right there and then. That would relieve you from getting involved in any disputes or disagreements between two parties.

Can you imagine if you recommend one professional and then your client did not like the service provided? That could reflect on you. Far worse, it may even result in getting into relationship conflicts.

But if you must recommend a professional, make sure you write a disclaimer. Such a disclaimer should relieve you from any liability or obligation. That should state that you will not be responsible (nor take credit) for the outcome from the transaction that is outside your professional real estate agent's duty and expertise.

As suggested, give your clients the list that they can obtain online and let them decide for themselves. In case of some legal challenges between your clients and the other service provider, you would relieve yourself from that responsibility. That you are not instrumental for introducing one party to the other and vice versa.

You must remember, as a real estate agent, you have your defined legal and moral duties. Such duties can, in some cases, be complex and challenging. So, it is imperative to focus on a real estate agent role and advance your knowledge.

If there is anything in which you find you lack knowledge, you may seek the help of your managing broker.

It is paramount that you let the broker know what's going on with you or on your situation, about your transaction, your activities, your relationship with your clients, and anything else related to a transaction, and even legal concerns and agreements.

You must never assume that you have all the answers. If a client asks you (or a prospective buyer asks you) about a property (and many other things) and of which you are not so sure, it would be better off to be upfront and honest. You could say that you do not know the answer. But that you will try to find an answer or solution to the best of your ability.

You should document every step and action that you do. In some cases, you may need to get some more information. You may need to request documents related to a property on which you deal.

You may need to address the problem that may require consultation with other professionals. That may include lawyers, accountants, appraisers, inspectors. And even at times, you may need to deal with government authorities and some city officials.

As a real estate agent, you must adhere to and maintain professionalism. You must keep up with a trustworthy reputation. You must continually have sound industry knowledge.

CHAPTER 8

Being a Professional Real Estate Agent

Being a Professional Real Estate Agent

Being a professional real estate agent means dedicating yourself to establishing a name and authority in your chosen market or niche. Achieving that objective is not just a one-time activity in which you could hope that it would do the rest. It takes a continuous process. You could look at a longer horizon if you are committed to creating your professional brand.

The moment you decide to embark on a real estate agent profession, you must be aware that you will need to go through some stages of preparation.

Technically, an aspiring real estate agent will need to undergo some training, including completing real estate courses. Some agents go on formal education to obtain a post-secondary diploma.

Real estate agents may decide to focus on the buying and selling of real estate properties. Or they may specialize in rental or leasing services (on behalf of clients). They may focus on residential real estate services. Some real estate agents, however, may pursue a commercial real estate specialization.

So, after completing the required real estate courses, an aspiring real estate agent would then need to take and pass an examination. After which, a real estate agent can get a licence. The licence would enable a real estate agent to provide real estate trading services or any specialized services that an agent can perform.

Once all the requirements are complete, you can then look for a real estate brokerage. In that way, you can operate and start your real estate practice.

You should know if the real estate company you are joining is a good match for you, considering your goals and resources. Then, see to it you follow and adhere to the rules and the laws and regulations in your industry and jurisdiction. Real estate licensing may vary. And that is, depending on which country, region, state, or province you live or operate your business.

With all the preparation you have had, you probably would not think of your real estate profession as a hobby or side gig, would you?

A real estate agent, although a part of a real estate brokerage, operates independently. You will have to treat your real estate trading practice as a business the way entrepreneurs treat a business.

A real estate agent must look at the real estate practice as an entrepreneurial venture. And also all other aspects that go with running and operating an enterprise.

CLIENT RELATIONS AND CUSTOMER EXPERIENCE

Clients value professionalism, and therefore, expect that real estate agents render professional service and client care.

Running a real estate business in this digital age has opened several opportunities, as well as several challenges. If you build a reputation for providing reliable services, you could have a growing customer referral list. What you have to do is start with one satisfied, happy client. Let that happy client be your ally in helping spread the word about your service. You may even request a testimonial and let the client speak for how good you are in meeting their needs.

But what happens if that client is not happy? And worse, your client can be ultra disappointed with the service you provided? How would it affect your real estate business?

If you mess up and neglect the needs of your clients, the effect could be disastrous. And that may ruin your reputation. Imagine how easy it can be to leave reviews on various social media sites. That would include Facebook and Google, not to mention other review sites and online directories. In simple, easy clicks, anyone can create user-generated content to publish online. You would not want that, would you?

Therefore, it is paramount to plan carefully in going about your business activities and see how you can deliver with clients' expectations with utmost care. Sometimes, you can find that a client seems not happy. In such a case, you should talk to the client and see what you can do.

Effective communication can help you go a long mile in the real estate business. Learn how to approach your clients properly by listening to what they tell you. Then, find the solutions that would match their needs. Providing real estate services is not a one-size-fits-all thing. It requires digging deeper or so, to say going the extra mile.

What could you do to make clients appreciate the idea that you have the sincere goal of helping them out with finding the right solutions to their needs?

WHAT DOES IT TAKE TO BE A PROFESSIONAL SERVICE PROVIDER WITH WHOM CLIENTS WOULD LIKE TO DEAL

As a real estate agent, it would take an approach that is dynamic and client-centered. And that should help to grow yourself as a professional real estate agent.

Know how you can gain more knowledge in your profession. Successful real estate agents must be aware of the current market trends. And they should continue to learn about all matters in their real estate practice.

You can create a support system that can help you with your marketing activities. You can join an organization that could help provide market insights in which you specialize.

If you are a part of a sales team, you may want to request a coaching session, if possible. Some real estate brokerages provide some training sessions. That can include sales training and even one-on-one coaching. Some real estate experts would seem happy to share their experiences. They could even share their stories and their successes.

As a professional real estate agent, it is imperative to know and understand by heart what the real estate sales process entails. That would include some activities from prospecting to presentation and negotiation, and of course, closing the sale.

You must find the time to hone your skills. You must keep trying. Until you could see things are starting work for you. As though they are second nature to you. You could also attend some classes, take online courses, and read some helpful resources. That would help constantly sharpen your skills and be ahead of your competition. You would know some marketing strategies and tactics that you can apply or integrate with your overall strategic marketing plan.

Next, it is imperative to understand and explain (to your client) the legal aspects that come with the real estate transaction. As a real estate agent, you must advise your clients to seek independent legal advice where and when necessary. And even other professional help.

Do not assume responsibilities that are outside your expertise. If you are unsure, you may want to check with the managing broker of your company or branch so that you can address a specific situation. Not all real estate transactions are alike.

Clients come from different backgrounds and cultures. You must understand and respect boundaries and know what you should ask. In most cases, you must assess or qualify your clients. That would ensure they are in a position to decide in the buying or selling process.

If you are working or representing the buyer, you must know whether they have obtained a pre-approval from a bank or financial institution that will finance the transaction.

What would be the buyer's source for the down payment? Have they owned properties before? Or is it their first time to acquire a property? What is the source of their income? What kind of property would they want to buy? Is it reasonable, given their finances and qualifications?

PART FOUR

PERSONAL BRANDING FOR REAL ESTATE AGENTS

CHAPTER 9

Communicating Your Brand

Communicating Your Brand

IDENTIFY YOUR MARKET NICHE

Real estate agents, to be effective, must know and decide on which market they want to serve.

By identifying the niche that would match the real estate agents' expertise, agents could position themselves as an expert in their target market, given the demographic and geographic area.

Ask yourself, "Would I want to solely work with buyers? Or would focusing on home sellers be more practical, given my background and experience?"

Some real estate agents focus on working on communities or neighbourhoods, targeting specific streets by mapping the areas. Some agents would want to work on clients with specific age ranges. For example, some would focus on working with clients that are raising new families. Some would want to work on single female buyers. Some would work on clients in the age range of fifty-five and above.

Some would work on foreign buyers. While a few others prefer working with clients seeking to buy or sell recreational properties.

Some real estate agents would want to work with clients seeking to buy newly developed projects. Such projects may include residential projects like high-rise condominium buildings, townhouses, and single-detached homes in subdivisions. Some may choose to work on commercial properties.

But one very vital consideration here is the target geographic location that you choose. The closer you stay in the area you plan to serve, the better the chance you would feel at ease. That is to work on and achieve your goals.

After all, you would know the area by heart. You would be familiar with its proximity to conveniences and amenities for which the clients may be looking.

You can easily navigate your plan of activities. You can eloquently talk about the location. And the benefits of living in that neighbourhood.

In doing so, it would be a lot easier to establish yourself as an expert in your area.

You can ultimately establish authority and leadership as the real estate agent name upon whom could be trusted and depended.

BRANDING

Research and learn everything about your preferred niche. Brand yourself as the professional agent with whom buyers or sellers would want to work. Branding is about creating the image as the 'go-to professional' in the minds of your existing clients and prospective clients. Create a strategy, integrating both online and offline.

> *Branding is about creating the image as the 'go-to professional' in the minds of your existing clients and prospective clients.*

You should create a brand name with which a client or prospect can relate. In effect, they should see your brand name online. And that is when you, as a real estate agent, employ a digital marketing strategy that uses search engine optimization.

Homebuyers and sellers nowadays have a variety of options to accomplish a goal. They would look for a real estate agent to help them with their real estate needs. They can find a professional by using both online and offline channels. But, their first approach is to do their search online. People have access to internet technologies and mobile applications. By browsing and using tools and apps, clients can find navigating and searching online with much ease.

Given your web presence, you would have a better chance of getting found online.

Branding requires consistency and frequency. As a real estate agent working to establish your brand, you must execute your strategies and activities according to your plan. That would ensure that your name, website address, and contact details would be visible to the eyes of your target clients.

As your brand name continues to become like a household name in the neighbourhood you work with, you can then attract the right audience and even prospects whom you never even met.

Visibility is vital in creating that image as a trustworthy professional. Because you have established yourself in your niche, prospects and clients would more and more acknowledge that you take your real estate business seriously. They can recognize how well you are building a name for yourself in their neighbourhood or community.

COMPETITIVE ADVANTAGE

Real estate selling is a very competitive industry. As an agent, how do you make yourself different from the other agents who are also working in your target location and demographics?

You will need to define your competitive advantage. What are your strengths? What was your background? What are your unique skills? How can you differentiate yourself from a bunch of real estate agents in your area?

In other words, what is your unique selling proposition (USP) or competitive advantage over the other real estate agents in the market that you operate?

Would you want to market and sell with higher pricing? That could mean you offer your service at a higher commission fee to select clients. Or would you want to sell with lower pricing? That could mean offering a lower commission fee to numerous clients.

Would you highlight personal service with communication that could include tips on maintaining the home, saving tips, and personal finance?

Would you highlight your service with an educational approach? That could mean providing educational information on your website. In doing so, you allow your clients to access information with ease.

Would you conduct a free one-on-one session or information session?

BRANDING YOURSELF AS THE GO-TO PROFESSIONAL REAL ESTATE AGENT

When you are enthusiastic, and you strive to do your best in every project that you do, that can radiate to the people that surround you. Your clients and people you work with could see that quality in you.

And because you love so much what you do, your clients can recognize your passion and authenticity.

They can readily acknowledge your genuine intent to help out others with their needs. It will not take long before one or two clients of yours can refer new people to you.

Sometimes, you would not even have to ask for it. Clients can be willing to help out and refer new leads.

You just have to connect to them. The more people feel you, the more they will come to you. And that can multiply with more prospects and referrals.

People show their willingness to work with a person who is dedicated and committed to their profession.

PERSONAL BRANDING: HOW TO TRULY CREATE A REAL ESTATE AGENT BRAND

If there is one thing you have to remember about personal branding is this:

You are your very own tool. The art of making yourself the brand that speaks about you and your professionalism would start with your self-confidence.

How would you communicate that message to your audience (or your clients) in this digital age?

How would you like to become an authority or leader that would inspire others?

"You are your very own tool."

Personal branding is about creating the right impression about you. It requires some intelligent efforts to create an image. That is, to the minds of the public. And in your case, to your audience (your niche). It is about preparing and asking yourself some questions.

How would you position yourself? How would you emphasize your qualities?

How would you establish your credibility as a genuine person and a professional and knowledgeable real estate agent?

How would you consistently create that message to ultimately become the right real estate agent and the authority in your niche?

Building a personal brand can be an arduous, difficult task. Where does one start with creating the right impression? And can that be your winning formula?

There are different ways in which you can achieve the personal brand that you want to create. Be focused on your niche. Learn as much as you can about your ideal audience, your demographics, your clients. Create a persona of your target client. Be authentic. Remember, people can feel that.

Show your definition of success by expressing how you got back on your feet after failing at some point in your life. People make mistakes, after all. That is human nature. We can't be perfect at all times, can we? Explore that human side of you. Express your determination and drive to make it as a successful real estate agent. Be a good listener and reliable service provider.

Be a storyteller. Tell them your background. Explore how you got to the point of being a real estate agent. Why did you choose that career? How do you think you can make a difference in helping out and serving their needs?

Recognize the person you look up to as a model in creating your unique voice. Why did you choose that person as someone who inspires you? That you could state your definition of success.

Explore how you have helped others. Have you created an impact on a specific client? What was your experience? How did you inspire that person to act on a decision? What benefit did it bring out in that person or groups of people? Or you may post it on any of your online profiles, even on your social media sites.

Let the clients whom you inspired tell the story about you. What is their experience working with you? It is like allowing them to give their testimony and feedback. They can even create a video or write a note. Such client testimonials you can share with others and on your website and social media.

When creating your brand, make sure that you deliver the message (about you) with consistency. Create your slogan or tagline. That message should describe your qualities as a real estate agent. What makes you different from others? You should highlight that.

Practise what you preach. Make sure that you do what you tell others. How you describe yourself and all other messages that you communicate should reflect how you live your life. Do not send confusing signals. People will discover that.

And lastly, you can create some content you can write and publish. That you can educate and inform your audience on helpful topics. That may include web content, email content, and even ebook content.

Creating such content types will help sharpen your skills. That could also help in creating an image or impression (about you). That you are, indeed, serious with your real estate endeavours.

By executing a combination of tasks, you can create an impression about yourself. That you are a dependable, trustworthy real estate agent. And that you are in the real estate industry for the long haul.

PERSONAL BRANDING STATEMENT

What is your 'Personal Statement'? Or how would you want others to discover you? Who would you be in the minds of your clients?

How would you present yourself as the real estate professional who could satisfy their needs? How would your clients recognize such an image?

WHAT'S IN A NAME?

In real estate, you may repetitively encounter the word location. Agents would often mention that real estate is about location, location, and location. If that's the case, what then would 'being an agent' mean?

Being a real estate agent is about establishing your name as the professional agent with whom clients can satisfactorily work to achieve results.

The initial link between a real estate agent and a client could lead to a professional agent-client relationship. The foundation of which reflects trust and confidence.

You have to create, therefore, that brand that can establish a link to clients. And that would reflect such a sense of confidence and trust. And that would instill in the minds of the target market.

> *Being a real estate agent is about establishing your name as the professional agent with whom clients can satisfactorily work to achieve results.*

Real estate clients, such as buyers and sellers, could readily recognize a brand. They often search and find what they need online and offline. They can be familiar with some names of agents.

Some clients may want to know more details about a real estate agent. They seek information about the person before they even consider any presentation appointment.

Doing a real estate business, therefore, is about creating trust, authority, and leadership in the minds of the clients.

What does that indicate?

That would mean creating a strategic plan to establish and achieve that goal. Such a goal would be to position yourself. And to create a brand as a professional real estate agent with a touch of uniqueness. That you would highlight as you communicate your brand.

With thousands of real estate agents working and improving the buying and selling services in various cities and communities, how would you stand out?

What is the right approach to communicating your services to your clients? In other words, how does a real estate agent build a name and communicate that brand?

A BRIEF LOOK AT MARKETING

You must have heard about the four P's of marketing. That would include product, pricing, place, and promotion. During your planning stage, you must review such essentials of marketing.

The very purpose of marketing is to satisfy a customer or groups of customers (or clients). Therefore, marketing must start with the customer or client in mind.

The customer is at the very core of the marketing cycle. All other parts in the mix must blend well.

As a marketer, your goal would be to creatively use and combine all parts in the mix to meet clients' needs.

BRANDING AND MARKETING

Branding is not just simply designing a logo, handing out flyers, and promoting your presence online. Although, these activities can form part of the whole approach in branding.

Branding is about creating a strategy. That can boost your uniqueness. That can establish your competitive advantage. That can lead to establishing that link to your client. That can help you grow your professional relationship.

Above all, branding can help you communicate the totality of your intent. And that is to deliver customer value.

Now, as a real estate agent, you should seriously think, plan, and execute your strategies to establishing your brand.

Creating a brand would be to look at yourself and how you project to other people. There is a pre-conceived idea about how others look at you. Whether accurate or not, people have their impression of you.

When you think of branding, you can think of an approach in how you will position yourself. How would you communicate your intentions and get into the hearts and minds of your target clients? And that you can speak, truthfully, of the value of your service.

Creating a brand is to look at marketing in a whole, new, holistic way.

MARKETING IN THE DIGITAL AGE

Marketing in this era of digital media can be more complex than it used to be. There seems to be a reverse approach. Gone are the days when customers can just be passive and simply wait for what producers, product developers, or manufacturers can offer them. These days, customers are more active. They can even create their means to communicate through the use of social media networks.

As technologies evolve, we can expect to see more websites and mobile apps. Customers and clients have more options on which websites or social media networks in which they want to participate. They also seem to participate in many web forums and review sites. Many would create, if not, share user-generated content.

A few clients could have positive experiences. Some clients, however, could have negative experiences. Regardless of their experience, customers can, in a flash, talk about their experience. They can easily publish their comments.

That is how quick it would seem people could converse these days. Any video could go viral online, anytime. And people would talk about that. Many would read some comments on social media. That somehow could create an impact on customers' buying decisions.

But what could be worse if you do not give attention to your brand? You would experience some challenges in improving your online reputation.

Now, more than ever, businesses and professionals must actively work on their digital footprint. Hence, there's a need to focus on digital marketing.

A QUICK LOOK AT THE CONCEPT OF DIGITAL MARKETING

In my book: *Micro Enterprise Marketing: How to Start, Promote and Grow Your Micro Business in this Digital Age*, I explored digital marketing in depth. Digital marketing is, as defined in the book: "a marketing concept that aims at communicating your brand (product or service) through the use of a combination of digital channels to reach your target market."[1]

"Digital marketing is a marketing concept that aims at communicating your brand (product or service) through the use of a combination of digital channels to reach your target market." (Atienza, S., 2021)

---

[1]Atienza, S. (2021). *Micro Enterprise Marketing: How to Start, Promote and Grow Your Micro Business in the Digital Age.* Richmond, B.C.: Privilege Digital Media.

A real estate agent must, therefore, pay attention to the use of digital marketing to communicate the brand. If you want to thrive in this day and age, you must prepare to go digital. Everyone is going online, and so are your clients. Even your competitor may be online. So why wouldn't you?

In a report prepared by the National Association of REALTORS® Research Group called *"2021 Home Buyers and Sellers Generational Trends Report"*, we could see that majority of home-buyers or about ninety-seven percent (97%) accessed the internet (to search for properties). [2]

The said report from the *"2021 NAR Home Buyer and Seller Generational Trends Report"* further indicated how homebuyers relate to agent communications, in addition to the channels of communication, such as calling, texting, and sending emails. Some homebuyers would look into agents with some digital approaches to communications. That would include having a website and a mobile site to showcase homes. Homebuyers also started to look into agents being active on social media and having a blog. (NAR, 2021)

---

[2] National Association of REALTORS® Research Group. (2021). *2021 Home Buyers and Sellers Generational Trends Report*. National Association of REALTORS®. https://www.nar.realtor/sites/default/files/documents/2021-home-buyers-and-sellers-generational-trends-03-16-2021.pdf

In a 2018 CMHC study, homebuyers predominantly conducted research online, and only one-fourth did offline research. [3]

In the digital age where we are now, many homebuyers would conduct activities online.

That would include using mortgage calculators, comparing interest rates, and even accomplishing financial assessment and submitting mortgage applications (for pre-qualification and approval). (CMHC, 2018)

As such, real estate agents should focus on how to connect with their clients (in the digital space).

Real estate agents may even provide such digital tools and resources. That would encourage their clients and even other online users to visit their website.

Real estate agents should be visible online. They should create their digital presence. They should communicate with the target audience. They should use digital channels to convey their message. They must be client-focused.

---

[3] Canada Mortgage and Housing Corporation (CMHC). (2018, October 18). *Canadian Homebuyers insights: 2018 Mortgage Consumer Survey Results.* CMHC. https://www.cmhc-schl.gc.ca/en/professionals/housing-markets-data-and-research/housing-research/surveys/mortgage-consumer-surveys/survey-results-2018/homebuyers-data

In that way, you would know better how to thrive not just offline but more so, online.

And most importantly, you should work on your digital marketing with consistency to get found online with ease.

A REAL ESTATE AGENT'S APPROACH TO DIGITAL MARKETING

So, how should you go about with your digital marketing?

Similar to traditional marketing, your first step in digital marketing would be to identify your target market. It is the customer or client who must be the focus of all aspects of your marketing. That is, regardless if you are doing your marketing tasks offline and online.

As a real estate agent, have you identified whom you want to serve? Who is your ideal client? Can you describe your demographics? What is the age range? What geographic location are you targeting? What would be your USP (or your unique selling proposition)? What do you think is your competitive advantage?

Along with branding, you can include in your digital marketing a combination of many digital tools and approaches.

You may start to consider some forms of digital marketing, such as website creation, content writing, social media profile creation, social media content publishing, email marketing, local promotion, press release, and of course, video marketing.

Videos are gaining momentum. Many agents have used videos to promote their listings and their online profile. Many homebuyers have also seen videos as an added resource on real estate websites.

In video marketing alone, you can create different videos to showcase your brand.

BRANDING AND VIDEO MARKETING

The rise of videos on YouTube has amazed many people. It has been phenomenal. Many videos have gone viral. Video marketing has indeed shaped online communication and consumer behaviour.

So, what sorts of video projects should you create as a real estate agent?

You are, perhaps, familiar with property showcase videos. These are videos that pertain to Just Listed Properties, Sold Properties, and Open House Videos.

Producing videos, however, should not be limited to creating property showcase videos.

You can be more dynamic in your approach.

You can create Market Update Videos. That would show how many listings have sold in a particular location or community. You may even want to showcase each type of listings, such as single-detached homes market video, townhouse listings market video, and apartment or condo market videos.

Also, did you know that you can produce real estate web content videos? You can create a video project based on your previous content. That may come from your website or blog. The point is, you can repurpose content. That would even highlight information about which your clients or prospects may not know yet.

Then, you can think of a video project with a customized or branded intro card and end card. Or you might want to create a real estate business card video. That can be a quick, snappy presentation that can zone into your logo, your name, your expertise, and your contact details. In a way, that would work like a business card (similar to the printed business card). That will have your contact details. With a business card video, a client can conveniently reach out to you.

You could add the video (or a link to the video) in your email. That could go alongside your email signature. You can post the video on your home page. Or you could pin the video to your social media profiles, such as Facebook, Instagram, Twitter, and Linkedin. You could also include a video on your blog posts.

There is so much more you could do with video marketing. You could keep exploring your creativity or have someone help you produce the videos.

You could even think of creating videos in which you could invite your past clients to share their experience working with you.

Other video ideas may include creating and posting social videos for Facebook, Instagram, and YouTube.

How about thought leadership videos? Yes, you can think of some videos that inspire. You may call it an inspirational advice video. You may also want to create custom storytelling videos.

Another video marketing idea you may want to consider is a news-based content video. You can provide news, lifestyle ideas, and real estate market activities.

As a real estate agent, you can actively deliver vital information to clients. Your existing and target clients will thank you for it.

Real estate marketing is evolving way too fast. And as a real estate agent, it is imperative to keep up with the news and trends.

Creating real estate content or a news section on your website can boost your online presence.

With real estate news videos, you can have a starting point to generate content. You can share such real estate content with your audience and real estate clients. That will help you keep up with your social media marketing. And it will also keep you busy as you undertake your email marketing campaigns. Lastly, that will help you with your SEO ranking. Indeed, there won't be any limit to what you can do with video marketing.

FINDING VIRTUAL HELP

In working as a real estate sales agent, you have many responsibilities and tasks in your hand.

In between your consultation and servicing tasks (meeting with clients, showings, presenting offers, closing deals, attending to your client's needs, etc.) and prospecting (for new clients) tasks, you would have limited time for other equally important tasks. That does not even include your other goals. You may also want to think about growing your list of clients and nurturing your brand.

You may encounter even more crucial tasks. And if you do not give attention to such tasks, you may end up losing some prospects (or even your current clients).

You may not know it, but some of your clients may go elsewhere to meet another real estate professional.

You may need help executing your marketing tasks. Such tasks may include content writing, website updating, social media marketing, and of course, video marketing.

As your real estate business grows, your list of tasks would keep growing too. That is when you would need to find even more help.

Finding a virtual assistant, like a reliable marketing service provider, would just make sense. That would be your practical yet powerful solution.

In hiring a virtual assistant, you may search for a full-time assistant, part-time assistant, and even an independent contractor. That would be your call. And sometimes, that would depend on your budget. Better yet, you may consider working with a company that provides such virtual services. You may want to contact an independent marketing consultant.

In doing so, you could save time and money, not to mention, you may work with a professional who knows the ins and outs in digital marketing. You may need to create a job description that will outline the skills that you require to accomplish your marketing tasks and goals. You may need someone who knows about content marketing, video marketing and search engine optimization.

Such a virtual marketing solution would allow you to focus on your goals and your daily business activities.

Working with a marketing service provider would help you increase your productivity. And that may also lead to getting more leads (and sales).

PART FIVE

YOUR BRILLIANCE
AND YOUR
JOURNEY

CHAPTER 10

Choosing Your Journey

Choosing Your Journey

Are you up to becoming the next person with a million-dollar net worth? To some people, perhaps, that question is not hard to answer. In many cases, people dream of becoming a millionaire. Hence, the hopes are high with lotteries, casinos, and other money-generating avenues. People even join various contests on some television programs. They come with the hope that their winnings could lead to achieving some millions of dollars, or anything to that effect.

There is nothing wrong with thinking about becoming a millionaire. Somehow it is safe to say indeed some people made it with their first million dollars, if not at least half of that, or close to that amount. Some are on their way to reaching that goal.

Is there a secret to it? Or is there a shortcut to getting to where you want to go?

Anyone can freely explore that idea, depending on one's outlook and beliefs in life.

The whole point is, each of us has access to a varied set of resources.

But the difference, as what we have tackled earlier on, is a simple fact: setting the right frame of mind.

HAVE YOU CHOSEN YOUR PATH?

Have you chosen your path to where you want to go? What are your goals in the first place? Decide on your goals. Your big goal would be your destination.

Your small goals would be the steps that you would take on, and that could lead towards working on the big goal. Without knowing your goals, you won't ever be able to reach your desired destination. The worse outcome could probably be that you might end up on a destination that might surprise you, if not confuse you.

So why not bother, know yourself?

Know what you want. Know what would satisfy you in fulfilling the essence of life.

When you are ready to declare upon yourself what indeed it is that you want, then you are set to go onto your next step.

You will embark on your journey. At this point, you can decide on the path that you will take.

The idea is about choosing the journey and enjoying the ride.

That is about finding delight in your adventure. That is about knowing and understanding signals that come your way. You must know and decide when to pause as though you are looking at the traffic light signal. When must you decide to stop? And when must you start with your ride again?

You would probably experience some roughness and turbulence on the road. Yet the journey continues until you get to your destination.

CHOOSING YOUR REAL ESTATE JOURNEY

Many participants (in the real estate business) would want to pursue a profession in providing buying and selling services, with wealth as a motivational factor.

It is not surprising to see many people enter the real estate business with such a goal in mind. Some are mystified by what they could earn. They believe they could reach their first-million goal. Some would be happy to earn commissions with five to six digits of dollars.

With practically low investment to begin, considering the start-up costs, many people are attracted to becoming a real estate agent. They are aware of the possibility of earning substantial commissions.

There is, indeed, limitless potential with the real estate business. Anyone is at liberty to define how far one could go or would want to go.

If you aspire to pursue real estate trading services on behalf of clients, you must have essential skills to carry out the responsibility of a trustworthy professional. As a real estate agent, you must possess entrepreneurial skills. You should enjoy what you do and the tasks involved in buying and selling a property. That may include showing houses, providing consultative services, and meeting clients and prospects.

Real estate is the industry that will excite people who are passionate and who would like to explore consultative marketing and selling.

In other words, real estate is an industry in which people can embrace entrepreneurship. Real estate professionals are creative and motivated in working on goals.

Do you honestly believe that you will make it as a real estate agent? Have you found the answers to your questions (with reference to your goals) so far?

Did you know that it might just take at least one or two good questions to ask yourself? That is for you to be able to define the good answers that you are seeking? It is not rocket science. It is about exploring your inner self. Artfully.

Some people do not know what they are seeking, though. If they do, the good, simple questions would follow.

As a real estate agent, what is it that you seek? Then, ask the relevant question. For instance, you could say, "At the end of the year, I would like to earn 150K. What tasks must I do to reach my goal?"

Such a goal may not seem easy to attain. However, the moment you set your goal, you would, then, be motivated and focused on taking the steps.

You could accomplish your plans and achieve your desired goals in many ways.

First off, you must define your strategy or set of approaches.

Then, you must have access to, if not find, resources.

Consider your abilities and strengths. If necessary, develop your skills.

Next, you must acknowledge your weaknesses. You must assert your ultimate willingness to learn and grow as a professional real estate agent. Such ways would arm you to make it in this business.

Try to adjust or adapt to varied situations if you have to. Then, re-focus. And make your plan happen. Think of it as though you go through a cycle.

WHAT BRILLIANCE MEANS: A PATH TO SELF-DEVELOPMENT

To be brilliant is to acquire a radiant personality. That is as though the entirety of your being is shining with positivity. It is as though you embody the spirit of excitement. And that you always choose to be enthusiastic despite the trials that come your way. That would also mean you are doing remarkable tasks that are contributing towards accomplishing a goal.

To be a successful sales agent is to possess a brilliant mindset. But how do you think one could attain such a mindset?

We could mention at least three essential components to attaining a brilliant mindset.

In the earlier part, *Section Two: Achieving a Brilliant Mindset*, of the book, we mentioned such three components.

And these components would pertain to one, achieving a 'smart' mindset. Then, achieving an entrepreneurial mindset. And, of course, achieving a 'creative' mindset. Perhaps, these can overlap or can come in any particular order. And sometimes, one component can come as a result of the other.

Now, look closely at your idea of a successful real estate agent profile.

How does a real estate agent achieve an entrepreneurial mindset? How does one achieve a 'creative' mindset? How does one achieve a 'smart' mindset?

The answer to that would depend on how you look at your situation. And that would also depend on some other factors. That would include the environment, culture, family, values, opinions, and beliefs.

Can someone be born with a brilliant mindset, or can someone acquire it?

In a general sense, it is safe to say that one can acquire a brilliant mindset. At such a point, we have to differentiate fixed mindset versus growth mindset. Anyone can be in both mindset types, though at different times, from fixed mindset to growth mindset and vice versa.

The kind of mindset that you have could spell the difference. And how you would choose and take your journey.

In a nutshell, you could say one has a fixed mindset when one wants to remain with the way things are. The person might believe that there seems to be one single way to do tasks.

Perhaps, the person might have accomplished some level of success some time ago. And that person thinks that it can happen again. And again, and in the same way. And may zone into a singular point. And the person may not be open to looking into other scenarios (or possibilities). There, as the word fixed, suggests.

At some point in our life, or even in many instances, we tend to think this way.

It could be most apparent when we do not think things through many aspects of the circumstances. And we allow emotions to get into every part of our being. That could happen to anyone.

On the other hand, when a person has a growth mindset (as opposed to a fixed mindset), the person can look through the many angles of the current circumstance. The person can explore many possibilities through learning.

People who have a growth mindset can tap into their strengths. They can grow their skill set and abilities. They can explore the path (to growth). They can accomplish one step, after another, through perseverance. They are ready to stand up after a fall. They recognize the many roads they can take to get to their destination. They acknowledge other people's opinions. But their decisions are based on their sound assessment of their situation. They believe they can always learn. They treat each of their experiences as an opportunity to grow.

It pays to advance your knowledge. If you would want to do some more readings, Dr. Carol Dweck, an American psychologist, has explored fixed mindset and growth mindset topics through her writings to a greater extent.

ACHIEVING A BRILLIANT MINDSET AS A REAL ESTATE AGENT: A CONCLUSION

A real estate agent must make every effort to work on all the components vital to achieving a brilliant mindset.

In conclusion, a real estate agent must strive to work on being entrepreneurial, being creative, and being smart with their decisions and goals.

In addition, real estate agents must endeavour to work on keeping up with a growth mindset. If you are to pursue a growth mindset, you would welcome many learning opportunities.

People who have a growth mindset exert efforts and pursue preparations to develop the totality of their being.

They do mental preparation. They do emotional preparation. They do physical preparation. Such preparations would make up one's well-being.

In cases where one could feel weak (and would almost want to stop), think of all the preparations you have undertaken. Such preparations would help you turn to the other side of your being. That is to see the light amid the darkness.

Choosing your journey as a real estate agent would all depend on your mindset. If you choose to dwell on the growth mindset as you focus on your goals, you could be on your way to doing great. If, at times, you experience some fixed mindset triggers, take heart.

You could go through a process of choosing which way to go.

Every one of us is a work in progress.

Nothing is absolute as long as we keep evolving. That means you could keep trying. And if you ever would feel lost, you just have to acknowledge where you are. And ask yourself about your goals. "Where do I intend to go?"

Then set your journey. Tap into your resources.

Get on your feet and keep moving. And should you ever doubt again, do it, just the same. Keep moving, knowing where you should be heading.

All it takes, sometimes, is setting just one goal. From there, your brilliance will take you toward the next steps.

* * *

All it takes, sometimes, is setting just one goal. From there, your brilliance will take you toward the next steps.

BIBLIOGRAPHY

Bibliography

Atienza, S. (2021). *Micro Enterprise Marketing: How to Start, Promote and Grow Your Micro Business in the Digital Age*. Richmond, B.C.: Privilege Digital Media.

Atienza, S. (2021). *Savings Mix: How to Manage Money and Create Strategies to Achieve Savings and Goals*. Richmond, B.C.: Privilege Digital Media.

Canada Mortgage and Housing Corporation (CMHC). (2018, October 18). *Canadian Homebuyers insights: 2018 Mortgage Consumer Survey Results*. CMHC. https://www.cmhc-schl.gc.ca/en/professionals/housing-markets-data-and-research/housing-research/surveys/mortgage-consumer-surveys/survey-results-2018/homebuyers-data

Dweck, C.S., Holmes, N. (2017). *The Impact of a Growth Mindset: Why Do Mindsets Matter?: Two Mindsets*. Mindset Works, Inc.. https://www.mindsetworks.com/Science/Impact

National Association of REALTORS® Research Group. (2021). *2021 Home Buyers and Sellers Generational Trends Report*. National Association of REALTORS®. https://www.nar.realtor/sites/default/files/documents/2021-home-buyers-and-sellers-generational-trends-03-16-2021.pdf

ABOUT THE AUTHOR

About the Author

Sheila Atienza is a marketing professional and digital media consultant based in B.C., Canada. Before venturing into her marketing consulting and writing endeavours, Sheila has held a dual licence in real estate trading and mortgage brokerage.

As an author and content creator, Sheila focuses on marketing, digital media, real estate, personal finance, and self-development.

Some of her published works/books are available in:

University of Toronto Thomas Fisher Library; McGill University; Dalhousie University DAL Killam Library; Brown University; Library and Archives nationales du Québec; Canada Mortgage Housing Corporation; Medicine Hat College; Loyalist College; and other libraries across Canada and the U.S.A.

Sheila has authored several books in real estate, personal finance, and business, including: "Micro Enterprise Marketing: How to Start, Promote and Grow Your Micro Business in the Digital Age," "Savings Mix: How to Manage Money and Create Strategies to Achieve Savings and Goals," "How to Prepare to Own a Home in Canada: Recession-proof Lifestyle for Immigrants and First-time Buyers," "Canadian Home Financing Simplified," and many other books.

OTHER BOOKS BY THE AUTHOR

Other Books by the Author

Micro Enterprise Marketing: How to Start, Promote and Grow Your Micro Business in the Digital Age

Savings Mix: How to Manage Money and Create Strategies to Achieve Savings and Goals

How to Prepare to Own a Home in Canada: Recession-proof Lifestyle for Immigrants and First-time Buyers, *Second Edition*

Canadian Home Financing Simplified: How to Qualify as a Real Estate Buyer

Feed and Discern: Some Words of Wisdom, Some Poems, Some Life Lessons

NOTES